Arts and Sciences

Poems

Also by Allen Stein:

Your Funeral is Very Important to Us

Unsettled Subjects: New Poems on Classic American Literature

My Youth and Early Deaths

Arts and Sciences

Poems

Allen Stein

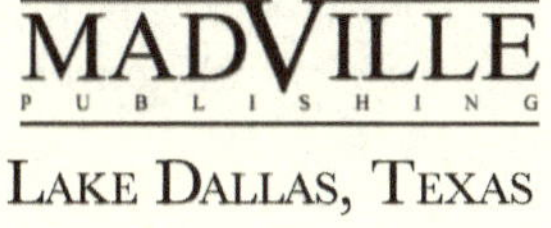

Lake Dallas, Texas

Printed in the United States of America

FIRST EDITION

Requests for permission to reprint or reuse material from this work should be sent to:

Permissions
Madville Publishing
PO Box 358
Lake Dallas, TX 75065

Cover Design: Jacqueline Davis
Cover Art: Johannes [Jan] Vermeer (1632–1675).
The Astronomer (1668). Oil on canvas (51 cm x 45 cm).
Musée du Louvre, Paris, France.
Author Photo: Connie Stein

ISBN: 978-1-963695-63-2 paperback
978-1-963695-64-9 ebook
Library of Congress Control Number: 2025946824

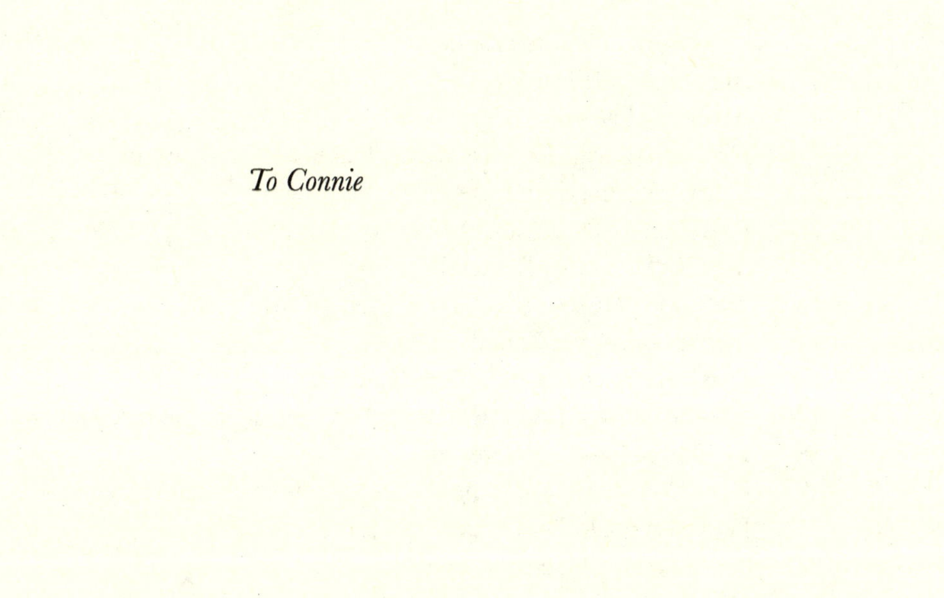

To Connie

Contents

The Arts

I

II

The Sciences

The Arts
I

Horatio, on His Late Friend

So, he implored me to, as he put it,
quit felicity for a time, draw breath
in pain and tell his tale to this harsh world.
No light burden. Toplofty eloquence
was always his thing, not mine. Where to start
in aching words for him and the dead left heaped
in his final scene, as fodder for the First Folio?
(He always played to an audience,
even when he walked the ramparts alone.)
No doubt, he would want me to pass along
his pseudo-profundity that there's more
in heaven and earth than ever dreamt of
in our philosophy. But who, except him,
ever thought otherwise, book-steeped or not?
That the libraries left out some matters
of note confounded him; though near thirty
he was, you see, still just a boy in thought,
astonished that a brother might smile yet scheme,
that a mother might be less than a saint,
that an unquiet ghost might walk of a night,
and certain that a prince thoroughly versed
in the subtlest texts of Wittenberg
could set all to rights. Now, *that's* a tale to tell,
of one by nature formed to turn all he touched
to chaos. Of course, he could be fun
once you got past all the self-absorption
and drama prince stuff—had a wicked wit—
the "country matters" pun with poor Ophelia,
the clouds of camel, whale, and weasel
with Polonius, the clowning with R&G—
lots of laughs till they all became corpses.
He was a pendulum, one day pallid
and ill with thought and the next impatient
to take arms against his sea of troubles.
It's not like I didn't tell him, more than once,
"Look, Hamlet, either go tell Claudius
what goes around comes around, stick a blade
in his gut, and be done with it, or shrug,
let it go, and tell yourself the bastard

is sucking in bad karma with each breath,
because right now you're getting nowhere."
He'd nod, brood, then stalk off, hunched and muttering.

Now, broad-chested Young Fortinbras, chin raised,
soldiering in last night to wipe the boards clean,
is somehow shaped of different stuff,
born to deal with the business at hand.

So, my tale concludes inconclusively.
What a piece of work is man indeed.
Consider this Hamlet, formed of two arms,
two legs, head and heart, like any other man,
but unaccountably out of joint with time
and circumstance, a life to put all thought
of choice to rout, each sprocketed wheel
and linked chain fine geared to go its set course
toward an end unanticipated
in all we'd read and, yes, sweet prince, undreamt
in my philosophy. To what purpose,
a Hamlet? To what purpose, as he himself
might ask, an *anyone*, as each is placed
here to hit his marks on this ancient stage
under the cold and silent stars?

Ishmael in Safe Harbor

Lone survivor, back on land, his tale told,
he walked with a rolling gait, as if still
keeping balance on a pitching vessel
or beating through heaving seas of his mind.

He married after a time, a plain girl,
patient and forbearing both with his hypos
and his unsettling exuberances.
Beside her in the dark under the bedclothes
he sometimes felt less alone, but never
conjoined as at the Spouter Inn
with the brown-skinned harpooner.

Through long clerk-days at the bank, tallying
accounts under a flickering oil-lamp,
there were hours when he seemed to himself
becalmed, as if awaiting a breeze
to set him sailing unquiet waters once more,
and with equivocal feeling acknowledging
it would never come again.

He often felt Ahab's tutoring eye
upon him, urging him to thrust
through the pasteboard mask of things,
to be grand, ungodly and godlike,
and strike both the insulting sun itself
and whatever placed it in the heavens
and set the white whale upon the waters.
At those moments, the beat of his heart echoed
the relentless tread of a whalebone leg
on the oaken planks of the *Pequod*.

But days were frequently clear and the climate
temperate and the church bells chimed
the old notes of solid assurance and humility.
And the times of hardtack biscuits,
of beans and salt beef, of bloody shark steak,
seemed of another life as he sat to Sunday dinner
and looked across a spotless white tablecloth
at his mild, smiling wife, and began to carve.

It was a rare Sabbath afternoon that, arm in arm,
he didn't walk, smiling with her, along the Battery,
where the rivers met, and buy her a chocolate
or an ice. Sometimes, though, as clouds billowed in waves
on the horizon, he'd look out to the bay and beyond,
and then he'd turn from her, so she wouldn't see
the tears in his eyes, the crucifixion in his face.

Ahab in Afteryears

In afteryears, he would climb to the widow's walk
atop his New England foursquare and pace,
hands clasped behind his waist and look to the east.
He wished the level planks under his feet might rise
and fall, as if on heavy seas. Pausing, he'd lift
a spyglass or place his hands on the railing and lean
toward the water, his face a torment of yearning,
eager to sail or sink—it hardly mattered which—
just so long as he could hear once more the tread,
measured and irregular, of his thick leather boot and his solid ash peg
on the oaken boards of the *Pequod* under billowing canvas,
while he pursued what had dismasted him, that white wall
or pale pasteboard mask twixt him and the vast Unknowable
he would risk perdition itself to know.

Heeding at last decent, dutiful Starbuck and the tug
of the common ties, hearth, bed and bride, he had turned,
and before a constant leeward wind sailed swiftly
under clement skies home to Nantucket, his crew marlin-quick
to consign the wild pursuit to cloudy memory. His final crew.
He brooded on the mates. Brave Starbuck now a chandler,
content to count inventory and haggle over coin.
Fearless Stubb, wed to a plump, moneyed widow,
and singing rollicking tavern songs when not jumping
to the whims of his be-flounced and be-frilled wife.
And plucky thoughtless Flask, watchman at a wage-slave mill,
his dim lantern and flickering cigar-end the sole companions
of his empty night-hours. Better had the three gone down
seeking and striving, these common men of common sense,
with their uncommon captain, the grand ungodly godlike.
Of the rest of his crew, he knew nothing. Likely scattered
among the merchant ships, whalers, and grog shops.
Ashore, afloat, or at the bottom of the sea, they were lost
to the turbid depths of this fallen world. He cared little
for this human flotsam. He feared himself mad. Yet believed
that those who had never known moments of madness
carried but a spoonful of brain.

Neither his wife, widowed in all but fact,
nor the child of his old age dared join him
as he paced and gazed seaward,
for they sensed he was still voyaging,
outward-bound, with no thought of home.

Herman Melville Reviews Desert Places for Trip Advisor

"Traipsing the rocky barrens of the Galapagos
in a chilling mist, tasting ash in their brackish pools,
watching the ever-abiding reptiles trudge and slither,
I knew the chief sound of life here to be a hiss.
Such islands can exist in no world but a fallen one.
These ghastly cinder-heaps far off the coast of Peru
are a five-star destination solely for those so frivolous
as to find in desolation and darkest intimations only novelty.
If you have brain to think and mind to feel, visit at your peril!"

"At the Grand Canyon, I gazed into the Abyss.
I rate it a galaxy of the indifferent stars
for the mere gapers, zero for plumbers
of the depths."

"Death Valley is a placeless place, a nothing
in the middle of nowhere. An empty litterbox
in the vacancy. Enough to make one doubt
there's a God who gives a damn enough
even to damn us. It's a void
into which all stars are swept."

"Of Red Rock National Park, I can cite only
the disappointment of others on the tour,
who reported the colors 'faded, lackluster, so unlike
the pretty pictures online.' I preferred not to go,
instead strolled the sunless, smoky dens of Las Vegas,
watching crowds grin, blanch, or pray
at the turn of a card, the roll of the dice,
the slowing circulation of a small ball in a wheel.
I mused on nothing, mortally certain that the nothing
that happened in Vegas never stayed merely in Vegas."

I Hear Negatively Impacted America Singing

"I hear America singing, the varied carols I hear."
—Walt Whitman

"We're shifting some divisional structures to better align with our corporate priorities…"
—SAS spokesperson announcing firings, July, 2023

I've been negatively impacted by a shift
of divisional structures. I'm no longer aligned
with corporate priorities, terminated
as the company drives down its headcount
incrementally.
                    Whitman heard the songs
of the carpenter at his plank, the blacksmith
at his forge, the mason at his wall.
No songs from us, the terminated,
who long since have had too narrow a bandwidth
for language or melody. What words for hours spent
eyes glazing at a screen, for long-range strategy meetings
that leave the taste of Styrofoam, weak coffee,
stale bagels and dry Danish on the tongue?
What tune for watching a learned marketer
aim a flickering laser at a list of powerless points
or for chuckling along with assembled "associates"
at the CEO's belabored facetiousness and for feigning
orgasmic joy at the rollout of a gadget's eighteenth incarnation?

So, now that they've moved the goalposts on us,
that major game-changer, that proactive
paradigm shift more robust than we had anticipated,
being as far out of the loop as we were,
(perhaps best practice for the firm, though, going forward),
we're basically blindsided, thrown under the bus,
with no leverage, no possibility of gaining traction
or moving the needle. Unempowered by the empowered,
unvalued within the contextualized framework
of the company's core values, we long to sing a song
of efficacy that can bring to the table a new dynamic,
but at the end of the day, we whose heads
did not survive the cut of the corporate blade
can do nothing but drone the drone of drones.

Below Emily Dickinson's Window

> After Dickinson withdrew from the outer world, she would often lower a basket of treats to children who had gathered in the garden below her second-story bedroom.

We would never see more than her pale hand
and thin wrist, cuffed in frilly white,
reaching from behind a gauzy curtain
and holding one end of a rope. We'd gather
in the garden beneath her bedroom window
when the smell of baking drifted from her kitchen,
sweet as early spring, but never without a hint
of the leaf burns of fall, or so it seemed there
in the shifting dappled shade of the elms.
We were children eager for the ginger cookies
and thick slices of Black Cake she'd lower gently
in a worn basket of dark willow wicker
sharp in spots with strands that had worked
their way loose over time. We boys cared little
for the flowers in which she wreathed the treats,
though the girls would set them in their waistbands
or drape them over an ear and wonder if they looked
as fetching as they imagined the unseen Miss Emily.
As she herself knew, the slow fuse of the possible
often takes fire in the fancy. Scattered sometimes
among the blossoms and pastries were scraps of verse
that we could make little of if we took the time
to give them a glance. We were young,
so what issued from her brain and spirit
meant far less than what came from her oven.

Years later, when we finally read her lines,
perhaps over a tart wine under a flickering lamp,
we recalled the pastries we'd devoured
in the shifting light of her garden and knew
the communion she'd long sought was at last achieved.

Mrs. Richard Cory Remembers

It's the poem that brings them, of course.
Poor doomed Dickie, terminally aloof,
and something, frankly, of a terminal bore,
has become The Elegant Man of Mystery
merely by putting a bullet in his head
to meter and rhyme. "Why," they ask me,
as they're still panting from the climb
up Cory Hill, "Why did he do it? Surely,
you'd know," as if anyone has ever known
another since the world began.

Robinson's inventory of the man
made them long to be in his place.
Now that lading list for his voyage
into the dark, one calm summer night,
makes them yearn to be Dicky's intimates
after the fact, whether or not they'd ever
been brushed by his all-purpose smile
as he passed, glittering, on the street
or had their pulses fluttered by the gleam
of his impersonal "Good morning."

How little being his intimate had to offer.
There was simply nothing there. He'd sit
on the verandah and stare down at the waves
that dashed against the boulders far below,
then fell back and dashed themselves again,
and he'd sigh and mutter "Metaphorical"
and stare some more. Of an evening, he'd gaze
at the fire, magazine in lap, smile wanly, and say,
"I could write a verse about that flickering glow."
Then he'd yawn, "Yes, I really should."

Had Robinson actually met him, his poem
might have asked why I hadn't long since
put a gun to my own head or even spared Dickie
the effort of raising the barrel to his. Oh,
how he loved the shy greetings and bashful grins
that told him he was indeed admirably schooled

in every grace. But, finally, they just weren't enough,
I suppose, and even self-admiration failed him at the end.

What would have been enough, I can't say.
And I suspect he couldn't have, either.
Reflection was never his long suit,
and, clearly, neither was endurance.
In Robinson's words, most go on,
waiting for "the light," whatever
that might be. Not Richard Cory.
As Dickie turned off the lamps
that final night, he spoke his last words,
the ones he'd spoken nearly every bedtime
of our marriage, "Well, another day,
another dollar." And that was that.

I tell the callers to make of it what they will,
or to ask Edwin Arlington Robinson.
If there are answers, I don't have them.

The Song of the Mermaids (A Recollection)

> "I have heard the mermaids singing, each to each. I do not think that they will sing to me."
> —T.S. Eliot, "The Love Song of J. Alfred Prufrock"
>
> "If the mermaids can't sing to me here, Christ, they never will."
> —Marlon Brando, in Tahiti

I heard the Mermaids singing
each Saturday night that summer
at Mike Angelo's South Seas Paradise.

On a half-deserted dead-end street,
behind doors of splintering bamboo,
spindly potted palms and rusted anchors
sat on linoleum in sand and sawdust.
Lacquered swordfish hung in nets
on spackled walls, and in shadowy corners
lobster traps squatted far from the tiki torches
and the soft beam of evening indigo
that spread out against the ceiling
like an unstirring lagoon.

Sinking into cushioned frayed rattan,
filling oyster-shell ashtrays with Luckies
smoked to the butt-ends, catching whiffs
of two-bit stogies and overripe pineapples,
I drained Mai Tais and Margaritas
and swelled with yearning, three Bronx bus-stops
from Orchard Beach, with its waves ankle-high
and tepid and its hazy view of Hart Island,
where New York's unknown dead lay three-deep
in more than a million unmarked graves.

The Mermaids, a quartet just past their teens,
powdered, mascaraed, bouffanted,
silver-shimmery in tight low-cut gowns,
sang "Heat Wave," "Surfer Girl,"
and "Will You Still Love Me Tomorrow?,"
their arms reaching, imploring, in time

to their shining swaying hips.
The second from the left met my glance
one Saturday with what seemed an inviting smile.
I'd seen the wan faces of lonely men
in subways, staring at the *Daily News*
as they rode toward frozen dinners
and TV screens, and I feared for the future.
So, though my arms and legs were thin
and my hair dwindling, I dared finally to speak.

That was ages ago. In Florida now,
I sip Bud from a bottle, gaze
out to sea and hear only the surf.
She stopped singing to me
long before she left.
She sat and chain-smoked,
her face gone hard,
her voice gone scratchy,
her glittery stage-gowns yellowing
in the bedroom closet.

It's been years since I've heard from her.
She may be under the waves I watch,
in a place where she's turned pale blue
and scaly, drifting in the darkest depths
till she rises bright and glistening once more,
from another sea, to sing her song
to another unlucky listener
on another unlovely shore.

Inscriptions (after Kafka)

Long ago, in the penal colony, guilt was a given.
The old Commandant's sharp-edged machinery
of justice ripped skin into scripture, the body itself
into a gouged and torn object lesson of violation's wages,
till, at last, the deep-cut words bled enlightenment
even to the dimmest. Now, the old Commandant is gone.

Yesterday, in the Ministry of Due Process, my co-workers
left their desks early, it being the eve of the weekly TGIF revelry,
their open ledgers showing the daily smears, stains, and blots,
the ink-jet printers and photocopiers spitting piles of pardons
and commutations to the dusty, sticky laminate floor, the whirring
of the machines not quite drowning out the chirping and hissing
of my departing colleagues, the wheeze of dank air-conditioning
stirring their antennae as they waited for the creaking elevator.
Sighing, I put the nib of my fountain pen to the underside of my forearm
once again, and inscribed yet more deeply, as blood and ink streamed,
"Honor thy Father."

Daisy Fay Buchanan at Miami Beach

"Of course, Tom was unendurable when FDR came in.
Fueled already by two scotches neat, he'd sneer,
'Your daily dose of Bolshie tripe, eh?'
as I read the morning paper over a poached egg and toast.
More than once, he grabbed the *Tribune*
from my hands, balled it in his heavy fist,
and hurled it across the dinette.
Yes, as the campaign song said,
happy days were here again,
and a crumpled Roosevelt, his cigarette-holder
still clenched at a jaunty tilt, grinned up at me
from the linoleum floor.

We were in Queens then, everything lost in '29.
Nothing left even to gaze out on.
No sweep of lawn, damp with the early mist
drifting in off the Sound,
no dock with its glimmering green light.
Only a cement courtyard glimpsed
from a third-floor flat two blocks from the train.

Twice a week, he'd ride it in to Wall Street,
call our broker "a tool of Jew bankers,"
and beg to trade on margin, commission-free.
Then off to the Yale Club to cadge lunch
from anyone who'd still put up with him,
a quick stop at some stale-sheet whore house,
and his day was complete.
Still the hulking bore I'd married,
but bleary-eyed now, with fat sprawling over his collar
and no gilding of ready cash.

Over drinks at night, I'd stifle yawns
as he droned weary tales of touchdowns and tackles
and the time he broke the Harvard quarterback's arm.
When he'd start in about
'that presumptuous upstart from West Egg,'
whose name he never spoke,
I'd go to bed to brood and wonder
through the long hours.

The stray affairs I had during the thirties
mattered little to me or anyone else.

Just before the war, Tom's liver,
sloshing booze since prep school, gave out,
and the insurance got me my bungalow here.

At dusk, I like to sit and watch the ships
near the horizon, heading for the distance,
their lights dimming into the darkness.
Maybe one fine day I'll book passage.

Another Rose for Emily: Miss Emily Grierson, in the Late Hours

No doubt they'll chatter of me long
after I'm in the ground; and some author
may likely fancy he's told my story.
Let them. None of it captures me.

Father wanted a son. I was his sole child,
both Mother's fault and mine, his first glance
over breakfast each morning reminded us.
I recall fondly his last, gasping hours,
his eyes pleading for the painkiller
just out of reach. Mother, had she endured
till that evening, could not have withheld
his two teaspoonfuls. Unlike her, though,
I bore his blood in mine, so I showed him
his empty spoon, flourished it before him,
while the late-day sunbeams streaming
through the jalousie played on it, glinting,
as they might on bayonet or saber.
For three days, I did not give up his corpse.
All thought it grief's refusal to yield to fact,
not seeing that one does not easily part
with a trophy of hard-won victory.
The stink of decay was fragrant to me
as a heap of Yankee bodies to father
and Colonel Sartoris and all that brood,
who would kill and keep killing to hold
what God Himself forbade them.

Rebuffed at Shiloh, Chickamauga,
and Gettysburg, the men limped home, resolved
to lord it once more under their own roofs.
By breed and inclination one of them,
I chose at last to brook no man's grip
on my set will. If I could not lead a troop
across an open field, crying havoc
in my hot blood, I could, in the silent,
shadowy skirmish-land of my father's house,
wrap my closest foes in the embrace
that lingers even as all returns to dust.

Driving Mr. and Mrs. Stevens

> "He didn't carry on any conversation with Mrs. Stevens much about something."
> —Naaman Corn, chauffeur for Wallace Stevens

At first, I thought she couldn't talk,
but he simply didn't want her to.
She was lovely, yet her words made vanish
whatever he and the third passenger
in the backseat, his interior paramour,
no less silent, had created of her
as they'd sat in unfathomable communion.

In the rear-view mirror that first day,
the window behind her was a frame,
and what it encompassed became the world
that existed merely for her small singular face.

Cresting clouds shaped ranges of amber peaks
and purple gorges. Treetops glistening
from a brief rain that autumn afternoon
extended boughs heavy with red and orange
and sun-dappled in lavender and misty rose.
All this was backdrop enabling her features
to seem the sufficient what and wherefore
as I drove the winding road's dips and rises.

Then, at a bend, that day, as blackbirds cawed
among the sparse leaves of a failing oak,
she said, "I'm thinking stew for supper,"
and he answered, "So you would."
Neither spoke again on the way home,
and I kept my eyes on the drying pavement ahead.

Over Coffee, After Stoning

After her folks carried Tessie's body
under burlap to Bentham's Parlor
to be powdered and painted for the viewing,
some of us sat over coffee at the café
and shot the breeze on how the thing had gone.
Tess hadn't surprised us with her whining.
She'd always been a mouth and mighty quick
to look out for herself. Not having her around,
rattling on about her laundry, her dishes,
and whose wife got a "darling new dress"
and whose was wearing that "old, faded thing
with the stupid blue begonia pattern"
didn't hit us as much of a loss.
We agreed the finale went more smoothly
this year—better aim mostly, we figured—
Graves took a long drag on his Lucky Strike
and said, "Well, *Tessie* was the target, of course,"
which gave us all a good chuckle.
Then Delacroix said, "Old Man Warner, jeeze,
that creaky-boned bastard was in rare form,
spouting that horseshit mumbo jumbo,
'Lottery in June, corn be heavy soon.'
I bet even he don't believe that crap.
Are we some old-time Aztecs, sacrificing
a virgin to make certain the 'harvest god'
will bless our crops with sunshine and rain?"
Fact is, we don't know or care how it started
—hell, maybe it all began with Cain—
but we do know well the keen joy that comes
when you ain't the one about to be kissed off,
the satisfaction in the heft of a stone
in your palm, in the free and easy swing
of your pitching arm, and in hearing the thuds,
the moans, and screams. It feels good, sure, to be
with the rest, in something that goes way back,
but mainly you're feeling more *yourself*,
more alive, than on any other day
of the year, treasuring each breath you take,
so contented with things just as they are.

Harry Caulfield Remembers His Father

So, you probably want to hear all about
my lousy childhood and my crumby dad,
all that Holden Caufield kind of crap, right?
(Sorry, I couldn't resist.) Actually, as a father
Holden was better than you would have expected.
He'd always had a soft spot for kids—rooting for
his sister Phoebe to grab the carousel's brass ring,
putting his fist through the garage windows
when his little brother Allie died—
so he made the effort. And despite the smartass graffiti
panning him when his book made it big, he was no "phony."
The mockery hurt him. I caught him once at a mirror,
wearing the deerstalker hat he wore while he roamed
Manhattan after ditching Pencey Prep. He blushed,
muttering, "Bogus. Too much for effect." In his late years,
it was a throwback baseball cap he settled on,
the St. Louis Browns, chronic ne'er-do-wells,
who went defunct in 1953, not so long after his crackup.
Maybe he thought the cap confessed that he never
managed to catch any kids coming through the rye
before they plummeted into the self-deceptions of adult life.
But maybe it also proclaimed that still he was apart,
above it all, looking down from a high field
of waving grain and sneering. Phony? No.
But a bit too much for effect, once more? Could be.

His writing students thought him a whiny bore
searching irritably for something in their work
and in them that he never found. He knew
what they thought. Worse, he knew
that as the decades passed, highschoolers,
assigned his tale, were turned off, more and more,
by its innumerable petulances. He never
wrote another book, having already told
the only story he ever had.

Mom, the former Sally Hayes, stuck by him, till she left,
tired of his chronic fatigue with a world of disappointments
that included her. She remarried and finally relaxed.

He never tossed an unkind word at me, his only child,
however, many he flung at waiters and doormen
and all the women along the way who were not charmed
by what he fancied was his engaging eagerness for beauty.

The days in Central Park with him were not unpleasant.
He even played catch a few times, mainly, I guessed,
out of his sense of paternal duty. He had me wear
Allie's old glove, the one with the scrawled poems.
They were too faint to read, though the glove
had never seen much use. I suspected that my father
wore it himself sometimes while he sat alone and brooded.
He threw so feebly that I hoped none of my friends were watching.
But, as I said, he tried. Once, he asked me as we strolled the park,
where the ducks went in the winter. I said, "South,"
and he nodded and said nothing as we strolled on.
Every so often, we'd lunch there with my Aunt Phoebe,
never with her husband, an accountant, whom he loathed.

In his later years, he hardly left his apartment,
and when he did, he'd usually shrug and deny
his name when some passerby might spy him
and maybe ask for an autograph. If he ever did stop,
he signed himself "David Copperfield."

He confessed near the end that often he'd yearned
to contact Jane Gallagher but never did.
No doubt, he feared rejection or, perhaps worse,
bitter disillusionment with what she'd become,
or maybe still worse, the discovery that she remained
all that he'd ever hoped she was. On his deathbed,
he sighed her name more than once.

I'm probably just another of his disappointments.
After all, at school, when counsellors would ask
what I wanted to be, I'd say, "Just like everybody else."
I'm sure he found nothing much to build on there.
And my becoming a personal injury lawyer
seemed to strike him as simply perverse.

His last words, so far as I could make them out,
were "I always miss everybody."

The Billowing Overcoat

> "Only the billowing overcoat endures,everything else is contrived."
> —Franz Kafka, from his diary

Gray chill out of the northeast. I huddle
into my dark coat, trudge through ice-flecked sand,
and listen to the breakers. In a puddle
a dead tern, white breast frayed, wings stiff and fanned.

Out of tune, I hum "Me and My Shadow"
and wonder how long since I last saw mine,
if ever. All this perhaps metaphor, though
the sky's simply blank, the sea merely brine.

Never quite a bug, but never much more;
cubicle dweller, I peer at screens, wrapped
in my coat, cold, slouched in sallow languor,
nibbling, sipping, nodding, agreeing, trapped.

Sleeves swell with the wind, my arms heavy and tight,
I slog on through the dusk, and into the night.

Of Literature and Empathy

> "The idea that students develop a greater capacity for empathy by reading books in literature classes about people who never existed than they can by taking classes in fields that study actual human behavior does not make a lot of sense."
> —Louis Menand, Professor of English, Harvard University, 2022

I developed my capacity for empathy
in 1953, the morning they marched us
from our third-grade classroom, double file,
past the butcher shop, a calf's head staring
at us blank-faced as it hung on a hook (flies
on its drooping tongue), past the pool hall
where at all hours young cautionary tales leaned
against grimy walls or bent over faded green felt
in a smoky mist, past the hump-backed foot doctor
who shaved my arthritic grandmother's corns,
and past the storefront shul where my grandfather
and other ancient refugees prayed in a language
I'd never learn, then under the El tracks,
the trains rumbling, their flanges scraping the rails.

Still double file, we reached the projects
and a ground-floor room not much bigger
than Jakie's Like-New Suit Shop. Books
lined the walls, filled three narrow corridors
of scarred mahogany shelves, and stood upright
on tables, their jackets bright through clear plastic,
a public library, my first.

In ninety minutes, everything changed.
My schoolbooks, my sports magazines,
my comics had left me where they found me,
but a dog-eared, yellowed "Youth's *Ivanhoe*"
took me to the blood-speckled packed dirt
of the jousting lists and into armored combat
to free those clutched in the mailed fists of the unjust.

On the walk back, I wandered in and out of line,
turning pages, eager to sit alone and read.

Then, as we passed again under the El, the class bully
pinched the neck of the girl in front of him
and laughed and kept pinching as she squirmed
and pleaded. I was scared of him, but I imagined
how frightened the girl must be, how tight
the grip of his fingertips, like the hold of a rope
around the neck of a bewildered calf,
torn from its heartsick bellowing mother
and hauled to slaughter; I felt the pain
in my grandmother's sclerotic hobbling walk,
in the aimlessness of the poolroom loafers,
in the imploring prayers of old men at a small shul
in a foreign land, and I rushed forward
and slammed my copy of *Ivanhoe* into the back
of the bully's head, and as he turned, stunned,
I smashed it into his face, again and again,
till he fell to the pavement, crying, bloodied
at nose and mouth, as if battered by the mace
of a virtuous knight who had shown no quarter.

Asked by the principal why I'd done it,
I simply said, "I felt sorry for Suzy."
Years later, I might have added, "For the first time
I knew the moral power of a tale well-told,
of words well-wielded."

At Poe Cottage

It was there that he wrote "Annabelle Lee,"
his tortoiseshell cat on his shoulder.
It was there, too, that Virginia died,
shivering, under the only two blankets
they owned and his threadbare overcoat,
while he, in thin jacket and vest, watched
and wept. A tiny white farmhouse, with kitchen
and sitting room on the first floor,
study and bedroom, both unheated,
on the second, it stands still, as "Poe Cottage,"
a small shrine in Poe Park, that slight patch
of trees and grass with a peeling bandstand
(he so loved music), at a busy intersection in the Bronx.

Late one summer evening forty years ago
when the last teens had sauntered from the park,
the traffic lights signaled to empty streets,
and the closing strains of "Hit Me with Your Best Shot"
and "Hurts So Good" had drifted out into the darkness
beyond the neon of the corner tavern (The Poe Cozy Nook),
I pried open a shutter, forced a window,
and entered Poe's home, my right, I told myself,
as one whose deepest chords responded to his words
and his pain, his yearnings and his terror.
Little tangible remained of Poe's stay there.
Perhaps the bed may have been Virginia's,
perhaps the desk actually his, but there was no doubt
the silence and the darkness belonged to him.
After hearing the soft tread of my own wary steps
in each room, the low moaning creak of each stair
as I pushed off oh so gently to the next,
I sat, soundless and expectant, till dawn,
hoping that through the quiet stygian hours.
I'd come to know intimately there
what had both fired and consumed my idol.

And at dawn, as a city worker, singing tunelessly,
emptied the trashcans outside The Poe Cozy Nook
into the tirelessly grinding, grating maw

of a hulking garbage truck, I knew at last
what lay behind every word Poe ever wrote.

Leaving the cottage, I heard a lone bird
sound a single note from a meager tree.

One Kind of Knowledge

> "We pay more for some kinds of knowledge than those particular kinds are worth."
> —Henry James

I read "Tintern Abbey" on the subway,
picturing the enduring ruins beside the murmuring Wye,
sharing Wordsworth's sober joy as under the spiring cliffs
and quiet skies he recollected in tranquility
the coursing emotions of youth.
I was a sophomore, and books were my bliss.
My own emotions churned as I anticipated
my future self recollecting how much the words
in Baskerville Old Face conjured for me now,
their very shapes, the tiny curves, rises and turns,
forming Gothic arches, high crags, and winding streams.
Meanwhile, the swaying car and all those in it
were less to me than the dim lightbulbs on the tunnel wall.

Ahead, I was certain, Beauty and Truth
grew nearer with each turn of a page,
like the Pacific with each westward stride
of Keats's stout Cortez. In years to come,
I knew I would summon to mind stanzas
I'd travelled with an ancient mariner
across dark, seething seas, lines I'd floated along
into perfumed night, wing to wing
with a bird who sang in full-throated joy,
my memory a dwelling-place for all the varied harmonies.

Like a missed train, so many years lived
through books are gone since I sat that day
in the tunnel and read of the ruined abbey
by the river and didn't foresee
the many nameless acts of kindness and love
I'd leave undone, the enduring betrayal
of a foolish heart by the words it loved too well.

The Block

The steeplejack, arms flailing with his misstep on the girder,
eighty stories above the pavement, recalling his laughter
as his father tossed him high and caught him in broad, muscled embrace;
the English major, on a shaded campus bench, feeling a rough palm
clamp over her mouth from behind, her book falling to the grass,
"Beauty is truth" sounding in her head like the fading call
of a distant Vespers bell as she writhes and gasps;
the surgeon, sweating, his scalpel unsteady as he stares deep
into a chest cavity and remembers his red toy stethoscope
tickling his giggling infant brother.

So many in extremis, so many stories,
as over a second cup of coffee,
I sit stymied at my keyboard,
tapping fingertips tunelessly on my desk,
staring out on the narrow city street,
and recalling the days
when I would grip a thick number 2 pencil
with grubby, nail-bitten fingers
and scrawl words I loved
in notebooks lined wide as avenues.

The Touch of Stone

In the travel photos I show no one,
my fingertips touch ancient buildings,
no gag shots with me keeping the tower
in Pisa from toppling or Notre Dame
from coming apart at the buttresses.
The stones I touch were set by men
who left dim, close rooms each dawn,
hunched and aching, making their way
through fetid streets in all manner of weather
to the sites where they built beauty.

Those pictures of my hand meeting
the work of theirs shape memories
that, each morning, prod and shame
as I tap tentatively at a keyboard,
find only wrong words, and wonder
what Netflix is streaming just then.

The Academic Poet Reflects

I sink into the worn leather of my chair,
ease back into the soft circle of lamplight,
and read a poem of reminiscence, not mine,
certainly, but that of one who left home
in youth to motorcycle through Spain,
tanned and bearded, like young Ernest himself.
Savoring the earthy wine of the village-dappled
hill country from a goatskin flask
as he lay beside a tawny beauty
in a fragrant orange grove; gazing silently
at smoky frescoes through a mist of incense
in the churches of tucked-away towns
far off the path of the tourist buses;
cheering from the cheap seats,
with all the passion of the aficionado,
as the bull dropped to its knees,
the sword still vibrating in the fatal spot
just below the nape, blood pooling
in the mottled sand—the man who lived all this
finds words to recall it in tranquility
and to share it with me, who never mounted
a motorcycle, rarely left the steady comforts
of home, and chose to live at the speed of a child
warily testing his first pair of skates.

I'm the more fortunate one, of course.
Avoiding the searing glare of Andalusian noons,
the grinding fatigue from unsettled nights
in dubious lodgings, the precarious unknown
around each bend, I've nonetheless gone his route,
and others still more arduous, line by line,
down the countless pages I've travelled. Meanwhile, year
by year, I've strolled the familiar shaded walks of my campus,
and written of lives lived less temperately than my own.
If, as they say, the unexamined life is not worth living,
I take comfort in knowing I've examined multitudes of them
in print and contain them all, and, if, now and again,
in the hours before dawn, the brush of a branch
at my window or a scent on the breeze rouses a fear
that much has been missed and time is short,
I remind myself that there may be a poem in that.

Tea-Time for Tigers

"You like tigers and you like tea,
so this is a book for *you*," she tells
her daughter, as she hands her
The Tiger Who Came to Tea
from the top bookstore shelf.
The child sits on a tiny stool,
stares intently at the first page,
then the next and the next.

Liking both tigers and tea myself,
I put my thumb in the new *Iliad* translation
I'm leafing through and imagine plotlines.
The tiger, a Rajah just in from the Subcontinent
on his private jet, exhibits all the serene civility
one would expect of a regal feline,
presenting a bottle of rare vintage
(exuding subtle aromas of chutney and curry),
warmly praising the oolong and crumpets,
and, on departing, neatly devouring
the impossible next-door neighbor
who never *would* trim his hedge.
Or, more darkly plotted, the tiger,
pacing and shifty-eyed, hackles raised,
on the lam from the zoo, his lips twitching
at one corner, like Bogey's in *The Petrified Forest*,
slurps his tea, wetting his muzzle
and the living room rug,
and leaves a trail of cookie crumbs
and cigarette ashes from window sill
to window sill, before dashing off
ahead of the sirens. Grandma, his hostage,
screams as she rides the tiger, her thin wrists
gripped tightly in his maw.

The little girl, finishing the book, sighs,
smiles, and passes it to her mother,
announcing "I loved it," the story, I'm certain,
cheerier than any possibility I might conjure.
"It was so fun," she giggles, "when he ate

all their food and even sucked every last drop
from their faucets, and they were so hungry
and thirsty." She grins. Her permanent teeth
are starting to come in. As she walks off,
hand in hand with her mother, I turn back
to where I left off in a book clearly for me,
at the account of Achilles dragging the corpse
of fallen Hector through the dust
outside the walls of doomed Troy.

It Doesn't Meet Our Needs at the Present Time

"If I were Robinson Crusoe, I would write on my desert island."
—Jorge Louis Borges, interview, 1984

It's hard on my desert island, writing
with a stick in the damp sand. I'm at it
the better part of each morning, the breeze
fresh off the surf, the sun, just an hour high,
glistening and glinting on the light swells,
inviting a dip, a stretching of limbs,
a sweet immersion in the tides of life.
I'm tempted, but I keep straining the stick
through the resisting dirt. It's what I do.
Sweaty at noon, I stand, shake clotted muck
from my knees, shins, elbows, and look over
the work of my hours and hands. Being pleased
with it proves more painful than thinking it rot,
for rot needs no audience, but art, like the rose,
if it blush unseen, is wasted on the desert air.

Borges might enjoy writing into the void,
for he knew how many of his words
were now the world's, and to hoard a few
solipsistically might please, like an evening
alone by a cozy fire, a snifter of port in hand
and a Haydn string quartet static-free.
One imagines Borges' desert island
well-appointed.

Mine, though, is barren, my words picked up
by no passing ship, the incoming tide
sure to obliterate them along with any brief notion
that I've scrawled something worth a moment
of even my own sight.

The Unhealing Wound

> "To be a poet's poet is to hurt. To hurt singularly, to hurt incomprehensibly, to suffer a wound that never heals, a wound not meant to heal because bleeding is the very nature of this wound—it is a divine gift—it is the wound of a savior."
> —Marilene Phipps-Kettlewell, intro to Jack Kerouac's *Collected Poems*

My rotator cuff aches, strained it
raking leaves—my teenage son
too busy to be bothered. Hell,
if I were dating his little minx,
I'd be, too. (My wife's varicose veins
look like a roadmap to a place I'm tired
of visiting—hey, maybe I can work
that simile into something.) Damn
that arthritic space-bar thumb!
And my head hurts--eye-strain
or first sign of a tumor?
Did Kubler-Ross's list have "dread"?
Maybe I'll try another Xanax?
No. Can't get groggy. Got to dredge up
another stanza or two and send this in
before the deadline. Imagine Larkin
or Lowell using something called Submittable
and waiting months to read on a screen,
"Doesn't meet our present needs."
And neither of them had to slog
the endless stream of student sludge
seeping from Intro to Poetry Writing.
And it's not like I haven't appeared
in a couple of the better journals
or don't have something useful to offer
about my miserably materialistic parents
or getting my degrees at a soulless state college,
and marrying an adjunct in Women's Studies.
Maybe I'll take some Advil, but can't that inflame
the intestine? Ah, God only knows why I bother!

The Rising Scholar Touches Hawthorne's Desk (An Academic Fable)

He'd published a dozen essays on Hawthorne,
presented at fifteen conferences, sat on ten panels.
His *(Sin)Fully Oneself: Penance, Penitence and*
the Hermeneutics of (Re)Generation in The Scarlet Letter,
now in its final chapters, was certain to be published
by a major university press, to much academic acclaim
and as much envy, but this was his first time in Salem.

Three days into his stay, prompted by a moment's whim,
he strolled from his research at the Peabody-Essex Museum
to the Custom House, where Hawthorne, languishing
as surveyor, had imagined Hester Prynne, shamed her,
and yearned for her, while brooding on ambiguities.
The rising scholar didn't enjoy reading Hawthorne,
found his texts' tenebrous hesitancies too tedious
for words and his characters lugubrious bores,
but knew what he could make of them
as a thoroughly trained and increasingly recognized exegete.

The Custom House struck him as no less dreary
than a Hawthorne tale. A tarnished gold eagle loomed
forlornly over the rooftop balustrade and stared
toward the turbid slips of the deserted Derby Wharf.
Life here, he saw, already torpid and gasping
in Hawthorne's time, had now long since straggled
into extinction, just as he knew Hawthorne's texts had faded
into irrelevance except as the stuff of academic discourse.

Hawthorne's office was closed off by a low railing.
The Rising Academic gave it a glance, took a musty whiff
of the Nineteenth Century and turned to leave.
Inexplicably, though, as if driven by something
beyond his own will, he turned back,
stretched his arm over the barrier,
and set his palm full on Hawthorne's desk.
For an instant, he felt a sense of possession over the man
and all his works and thoughts, and smiled in satisfaction,

but before long, he felt something else,
a tingling in his palm that persisted,
intruding on his research at the Peabody-Essex,
that rose and settled in his chest,
where it abides to this day.

He never finished the book, concluding uncertainly
that all conclusions are tentative, clouded in doubt.
He found much in Hawthorne to ponder,
penned some enigmatic brief tales that found few readers,
published no articles, attended no conferences, sat on no panels,
and felt more than a bit abashed to have been an "Academic."
He was even sorely tempted at times to have an "A"
embroidered on the breast pocket of his battered tweed.

The Professor at Publix

Hamlet weighing revenge
is more real to me than the guy
in the Patrick Mahomes jersey
pondering the avocados.
Anna Karenina's wedded misery
disturbs me more than the shabby pair
wincing at the price of frozen pizzas
and glaring at each other
while their five-year-old wails.
And Ahab brooding darkly
on the imperious Infinite
feels more my kin
than the liver-spotted guy
in golf-cap and cardigan
baffled by the aisle signs.

Whether it's predilection or occupational hazard,
it can't be good for my soul to find typeface
of whatever font more compelling than the face
of the man or woman in a market or across a table.

I tell myself I connect by lecturing
of the beautiful and true, by reciting
words that mean so much to me
and so little to my listeners.
But nothing really connects
and I really don't care.

Instead, I'm enthralled by the story of myself,
in which the professor, unsettled briefly
by the thought his life is spent between book covers,
nods absently at the girl ringing up receipts,
as her eyes conjure his recall of a couplet by Keats.

What If You Gave a Reading and . . . ?

I

“You going to the Spartans’ game tonight?”
“No, I’m giving a poetry reading,
actually, at the bookstore four doors down.”
“Cool,” he said. “I never noticed it there.”
His wife added, “Hey, you just rhymed ‘store’, ‘four’,
and ‘doors’ and then said ‘down’ right after.
Alliteration, right? College English.”
She winked. “You’re a poet, and you know it.”
I smiled and said, “Not many others do.
I’m as unknown as a second-string tackle.”
(Their son, they’d told me moments before,
quarterbacked the local high school team.)
Nearly three hours of late-Friday traffic
had brought me here, eighty-five miles from home,
to this small town, and a wobbly barstool
at a crowded pub, with its dozen TV screens,
and this couple seated at my elbow.
Twenty copies of my latest collection
sat in my car trunk, a bold-point Sharpie
in the pocket of my standard tweed sportscoat.
I mused on Eliot dining at Oxford’s High Table,
Frost reading at Harvard, applause echoing
from the arched rafters of Alumni Hall.

“You here alone?” asked the quarterback’s mom.
I took a long swallow of Newcastle,
mellow and dark safeguard against reflux
of gristly burger and sodden cheese-fries
when, forty minutes later, I’d perform
my missionary work for the natives.
“Yes, I’m currently between wives again.”
“No kids?” “Nope, not a one that I know of.”
“Your poems are your children, then?” she persisted,
this mom troubled that I’d never see a son
of mine score a touchdown or sink a basket,
never see a daughter dressed for the prom.

I considered trotting out Yeats's old saw
that you choose between your life
and your art, but asked myself,
as I had more than once, what if neither
turned out to be worth all that much?
After a moment, the husband chuckled,

"I've gotta confess, I haven't read a poem
since college, but I do read stories.
What do you think of John Grisham?"
I weighed politeness and honesty in the balance and said,
"I *don't* think of John Grisham."
They didn't linger after the bill came, a minute later.

As they left, in their bright rah-rah sweatshirts,
I said, "Go Spartans! Slaughter the Athenians,
show no mercy." Looking back quizzically,
they said the game was with the Cougars,
and were gone. I ordered another Newcastle.

II

My twenty copies sat piled beside me
at the rear of the dim, narrow shop,
five minutes ahead of my reading, while
some fifteen people milled around upfront,
chatting, taking up books, giving them a glance,
and putting them down. Eighteen folding chairs
stood before me, empty. A handbook I'd pulled
from a remainders pile distinguished between
"hung" and "hanged," between "disinterested"
and "uninterested." I sipped lukewarm water
from the half-filled Styrofoam cup poured me
by the assistant manager, a kid working a solo shift,
and when it was time for people to get seated,
I watched as they all left. Smiling sheepishly,
the kid came back and said, "They just got beeped
that their big table is ready at the pub
four doors down." He and I were alone.
"Friday nights can be tough here," he told me.

I had the dry-rasp feel and non-taste
of Styrofoam still on my tongue. He offered
to take a seat and listen to a few poems,
though he admitted, “I never get much
out of poetry.” I thanked him but said
I’d pack my books and go home.

Driving away, I hoped the pair at the bar
were enjoying the game, among their townsfolk,
on this early evening of what was likely to be a long fall.

II

Lady Agnew of Lochnaw and the Wages of Love

I stride in, past the creaky servants,
the yapping Scotties, the old, drowsy Mastiff,
his slobber puddling on the parquet.

It's been a long journey to Lochnaw Castle,
but in her drawing room she's waiting,
Lady Agnew, in the lambent glow of mild afternoon,
wearing the familiar gown of shimmering white,
her slim waist encircled by a lilac sash
that drapes the gentle curve of her slender thigh,
and then dangles, swaying easily
with the light breeze from the garden window.

And she wears, as well, her look
of languid elegance, her penetrating smile,
at once appraising and inviting. It's all no less
than I anticipated, all a bit more than I can face
without fear that my voice will quaver
and my own smile quiver into a silly grin.
My traveling tweeds itch, my armpits are damp,
and, desperate to see if I've left a button (or two!)
undone on my fly, I steal a glance down,
only to see that her eyes follow mine,
the Gioconda smile intact as ever.
I blush (as who wouldn't?), but remind myself
that I've dreamt of our gazes linked
ever since her portrait so transfixed me
as I scrolled the John Singer Sargent website
over my Starbuck's latte one listless morning.
And now I've reached Lochnaw in 1892.

I take a breath and am about to speak,
when she says, "You're not the first, you know."
No surprise, really, though it's a bit disappointing.
It does offer a chance, however, for me
to declare that no other could have travelled
as far through space and time to reach her
as I, and that this is a tribute to her loveliness;
but before I can speak, she mutters,

"Gets to be a bit of a bore, you know,
having to perch here in this get-up
each afternoon and listen to the inspired inanities
they all fling my way.
Why, just two days ago, some fellow,
teary-eyed and gushing spittle, swore
that he was 'my Gatsby,' and I his 'lost Daisy.'
Really, whatever could he have been babbling about?
I nearly called Agnew down to toss him out on his ear."
(I'd had hopes of her husband being off somewhere,
stomping through the heather and shooting grouse,
whatever they are.) I sigh, and she does, too,
saying, "Ah, you see my point. Indeed,
we bear what we must to keep the old place up,
so be a good fellow and don't neglect
to pay the visitors fee before you leave."

Five Pictures from Hopper

I. A Husband and Wife View Edward Hopper's "From Williamsburg Bridge"

She shook her head, "So wistful, so painful."
"Why choose to read that into it?" he asked,
"I'm *choosing* nothing, I'm reading what's there."
"Too much troubles you, you know. Always has."
She turned from the painting and looked at him.
"Yes, but let's not get into that today."
"Good," he said. "Let's just get into the picture.
Why 'wistful'? Why 'painful'? Only a woman
at her window, looking out under a blue sky
and two small puffy clouds at bright rails
rising toward the span. If she's forlorn,
I certainly wouldn't know it. Why should she be?"
"I guess only the woman herself knows,"
she replied, "but *look*, don't you see, she's so alone,
as if the sole person in a city silent and still.
Not a thing moves. A ramp, but no car, train,
or cart comes or goes, nothing is bridged,
and she is caged by that railed fence.
And look, her building alone lacks a fire escape."
He said, "Well, she can always jump, can't she?"
"Don't be crude," she told him. "Then don't be maudlin."
"You men. Yes, she can jump, if it comes to that.
Ah, see how she gazes away from the bridge,
from the paired rails, paired chimneys, the paired clouds."
He sighs. "Look, she wants no connection. She'd rather brood."
She sighs in turn, saying "And sometimes brooding
is all one has left."

II. In Hopper's "Automat"

In Edward Hopper's Automat, no one
has an appetite. Why would they?
The bright bowl of fruit on the windowsill
looking at once faded and overripe,
dwarfed by the emptiness within
and the darkness without,
is as insidiously anodyne
as paintings on hospital corridor walls.
The radiator warms nothing,
and the row of reflected light globes
stretching above the stone tabletop
recalls the unsparing glare of the operating theater.
At most, across from an empty chair,
one can manage a small biscuit
before brooding over coffee gone tepid
and an indefinable malady gone terminal.

III. A Room With No View

A Visit to Edward Hopper's "Room in New York"

They sit there as if waiting for something to happen.
But it already has, and they know it.
Have they just come in or are they about to leave?
No matter—this plainly isn't working.
The three paintings on their walls,
others' notions perhaps of better times, better places,
are blurred, insubstantial, but the closed door
that rises and rears, slightly off-kilter, between them,
reaching up and out of sight, is solid,
its horizontal slats suggesting not ladder rungs
but bars. It even lacks a knob.
The window frames them in the inescapable,
in all that's unyielding as the stone column, the stone sill.
He leans into his paper, as if to evade the enclosing arms of his chair
(only the merest shade lighter than his wife's dress).
She bends toward her piano, and watches her finger listlessly

as it is about to sound a random note of lassitude.
On the interposing table, a doily holds nothing at all.

What is it that has happened?
We can only guess—it's their marriage,
not ours—but as we peer in,
our own shoulders slightly bowed in the blanched moonlight,
and face the unfathomable white of his sleeves,
the pallor of her arms, of her downward curving neck,
we perceive that the window is cropped on the right,
not to offer them a way out, but to draw us inside,
where we begin to acknowledge, as they must have,
the vacancy that can encompass two in a room.

IV. Hopper's "People in the Sun"

The cropped rectangular landscape before them
seems a movie screen showing an unchanging feature:
a flat field of dry grass, drab as wheat stubble,
a row of low hills barely distinguishable
from symmetrical pyramids of coal,
and an overarching sky of wan thread-worn blue.
Four of the sitters stare fixedly,
their long shadows cast behind them.
The white slab of patio they sit on, the white slab
of wall beside them, are as devoid of defining detail
as the scene they watch, and curtained windows
offer no glimpse of shelter from the circumscribing glare.

Behind them there's a fifth sitter, hunched over his book.
He and the woman in a hat wear scarves,
his the color of her dress.
Might there be something between them
that the fellow with his head resting on a pillow
oughtn't to be oblivious to?
Or maybe something between the book reader
and the blonde with face partially obscured,
whose dress also matches his scarf?
Is he looking for answers to the ontological whodunit,

or merely lost in a noir tale of cops and gunsels?
He reads on while the others gaze at the scene before them,
wondering or not about what may be beyond
the cropped screen under the hidden sun,
while the shadows lengthen
at the resort to which at last we all come.

V. The Hopper Nighthawk's Tale

I

It's late August, '42, the corner diner,
cup of coffee on the counter,
not much on my mind,
maybe something Sinatra sang on the radio
about meeting again, don't know where, don't know when.
Marge had gone back to the Bronx and taken the kid—
hit me like the Japs hit Pearl Harbor,
but not worth thinking about.

Meanwhile, Whitey's telling me about his wife's bum ticker,
how he hates she's got to lay there scared,
alone in the late hours,
him being night-shift counterman, and all.
I nod to show him, yeah, it's rough.
But I know it's just another story with no future to it.

I look across at this pair perched near the coffee urns,
the guy a tough-looking bird, his hat hooding his eyes,
the dame a redhead, a regular Rita Hayworth,
except near forty, gray at the roots and bad at the teeth.
Seems the kind that knows her way around a bedroom, though.
I'd tell her I could take her for Rita, but the guy is right there,
so not a peep from me—nor from them neither—
nothing worth their telling each other, I guess.

Then one last lukewarm sip,
I leave a dime for Whitey and his wife,
never even try to catch Rita's glance,
and I'm hearing my steps under the streetlights.

II

A few months later, though, I see
the four of us caught somebody's glance.
I'm waiting at the doctor, congested in the chest,
flipping pages in *Life*,
and suddenly this "Nighthawks" picture
stares me straight in the face.
This Hopper guy painted us that night, from the outside.
He caught me mostly from behind,
and I'm part shadow, part light,
leaning on my elbows and staring at my hands.
Then I read that *Life* says the picture's all about
"emptiness in an urban wasteland,
where not a soul takes wing."

I don't see that right off, but then I do.
Four people with nothing to look toward
but the ends of their cigarettes,
hunched, weighed down
by too much darkness in the night outside,
too much light at the scarred counter.
All of us as stuck as the two coffee urns,
and as pale as the wall behind them.

And there's no escape.
The only door Hopper put there
just takes you farther in.

I Stand Before "Full Fathom Five" and Muse

I stand before "Full Fathom Five" and muse
on myself musing into the depths long
and long. As always, I admire myself
for admiring art, even this mélange
of drips, swirls, and smears. I peer
at the nails, the matchstick, buttons,
coins, and key embedded in the paint,
like flotsam in a turbid sea,
certain the intensity of my gaze
makes it clear to anyone peering at me
that I'm in my proper milieu, not the sort
to get Pollock wrong. I watch a blond thing
slim-limbed in tight jeans glide up to the canvas,
sketchbook in hand, and scrawl on a fresh sheet.
Sidling over, I whisper, "Hard to sketch
from ol' Jack the Dripper, I suppose."
She turns and says, for anyone to hear,
"Calling him that might have seemed clever
for five minutes about seventy years ago,"
and goes back to her scrawling. I walk off,
out of the building and into rain-soaked streets.

At a corner, as I wait for the light,
my cuffs damp, my glasses filmed with drizzle,
I glance into a wide puddle, inches deep,
and see myself rippling among the street scraps,
a nail, a button, a matchstick, a key.

Bessie Smith and I in Lockdown

"Thirty days in jail, with my back turned to the wall,"
Bessie Smith laments, as I sit on a weight bench,
my feet, shoulders' width apart, on hardwood parquet
in my study-cum-gym, and strain a dumbbell toward my right bicep.
It's drizzling and chill, another dawn in the Covid lockdown.
I pant "thirteen—fourteen—fifteen," as Bessie moans,
"I don't mind being in jail, but I got to stay there so long,
so long" and I mutter, "so long" and feel I share her pain.

Orphaned, she grew up rough, singing for pennies on street corners.
Years later, between songs, she'd spit on the stage floor.
I sip some bottled water and, looking west, over the river,
from twenty stories, I see hollow factories, new high rises,
and, beyond, mile after mile, an impenetrable miasma.
I struggle to raise the weight I hold, and as Bessie sings
"The lamp is burning low, I never had so much trouble
in my life before," I think of the heft of the blues,
the burden of my self-pity, the general intransigence of things.

Did Sinatra Sing in the Shower?

Lathered in soap, did he belt out "My Way,"
alternately sweeping his washcloth in long glissades
and dabbing percussively as he owned once more
the song that was his signature? Did he hum
"September in the Rain" as the shampoo flowed
in warm streams from his scalp? Did Ella scat-sing
"Time After Time," tapping four to the bar gently
with a teaspoon, waiting for an egg to soft-boil?
Did she warble "Isn't This a Lovely Day?" as she buttered toast?
Did Astaire glide across his bedroom floor as he buttoned up
his shirt front, knotted up his striped tie, and eased into his coat?
Nice to think so. One's life of a piece with one's art,
one's work of a piece with one's pleasure.

Even Camus' Sisyphus smiled, turning his task
into his triumph. One can see him on a rare day off
strolling in the park, trotting to a small hill,
and on reaching its crest flexing, stretching, basking
in his strength, feeling the sun benign on his broad back,
on his extraordinary quads and calves.

Meanwhile, clicking rapidly at cubicle keyboards,
we chase cursors, knowing that away from work
our agile fingers will never surprise us
by suddenly rapping out a happy rhythm.

All Shook Up

"Do you swear you'll be this fine mama's hunk,
her hunk of burning love?" the justice asked.
He'd answered, "I *do*," and Lord Almighty,
he'd felt his temperature rising, straight up
to just about a hundred and nine.
Then the caped and sequined justice had twirled
toward her, not a strand of his black mass
of hair stirring in its gel, "And do *you*,
Luci, swear you'll be this stud's lovin' teddy bear,
to have, to hold, to hug him anywhere?"
She'd laughed, said yes, and, whipping a three-sixty
on the pointed toe of his high-heeled boot,
his dark glasses reflecting the fluorescents,
he'd pronounced them "Man, huh, and huh, wife, huh."
"Love Me Tender" oozed over bride and groom,
and they'd kissed, his hold hard at her ribs.
Released, she'd noticed dust on the plastic flowers
beside the shiny particle board pulpit,
then turned and smiled at Mia, who sat alone
in a front-row pew, long spindly legs crossed
at the ankles and swinging, hands in her lap.
Mia smiled dutifully, a ten-year-old
at her mom's third wedding, the only guest
in the six slender rows of Vegas' "Cozy Elvis Chapel."
And as her new stepfather crooned along
to "I Can't Help Falling in Love with You,"
he and her mom beckoned her to their side.
"Group hug," Luci said, and the girl joined them,
her arms around both, his voice at her ear
as he'd leaned toward her and patted her hip
with a broad pudgy hand.
                                        The janitor,
sitting on the entrance step, raised a Bud
to them as they'd left, and warned jovially,
"Now, don't go down that road to Heartbreak Hotel."
The couple waved from the car as with Mia
they'd begun the long drive home.

Sam Cooke Knew the Score

> "Ain't felt so good since I don't know when,
> And I may not feel this good again."
> —Sam Cooke (d. 1964) "Having a Party" (1962)

Sitting on the fire escape, the brick wall
still warm to his back, the June evening
easing into night, he ran his wrist
across the ribbing of his Coke bottle
fresh from the icebox and felt the cool
glide through the whole of him. He hummed along
while Sam sang at 45 rpm
and his friends danced inside. His girl
breathed into his ear, "We're havin' a party,"
just as the stars above the Bronx started to show.
It was late spring of '63, finals were over,
He was seventeen, and nothing could touch him.

Meanwhile, it was 8 a.m. near Le Tri,
An Giang Province, in the Mekong Delta,
230 kilometers southwest of Saigon.
Binh Pham, skinny and sixteen, hidden
in damp tall grass, lay on his empty stomach,
the sun, simmering already, seeming inches
from his throbbing head, the ground pulsing,
As the two M54 gun-trucks rounded the bend,
churning through rutted mud, he gripped his AK-47,
sighted, and, at the command, fired with the rest,
his shoulder jolting with the recoil.
It was his first battle, brief and triumphant—
every ARVN soldier a corpse. He grinned.
Taking a deep breath, he hummed
a few bars of "We'll Liberate the South," and
pulled out his creased photo of the girl up north
he yearned to marry. He drank from his canteen,
the sun felt milder, and he knew
that any enemy he'd meet in the years ahead
would come to grief.

On Learning the Last Phonebooth in Metropolis has Been Removed

How did he manage it? No matter his speed,
logistical problems abounded.
Once the doors folded shut behind him,
so little elbow room to wrench free
of his double-breasted jacket
and shed his cuffed, unpleated slacks,
to unbutton his Oxford shirt,
and undo his Repp tie.
(No doubt he kept his wifebeater on,
the undergarment of choice for those
with biceps of steel.)
And what to do with wallet and keys,
coins and comb, hankie, eyeglasses,
Swiss Army knife?
(No pockets to bulge un-aerodynamically
when you soar out to defend Truth and Justice)
And his shoes—brown wingtips, well-tied,
with hardly any wear—they couldn't fit
under the red boots, could they?
Was he ever spied sporting his fedora as he flew?
(Did the booth ever smell of urine?
Was it covered in splotches of graffiti,
often obscene?) Did he come back
to search (no doubt in vain) for his stuff,
or did he make a quick drop-off at the Goodwill
on each Superflight?

So, likely, he had to go out
and buy a new Clark Kent outfit,
top to bottom, after each flight.
On his salary as a reporter?
Did he occasionally skim just a bit off the top
before he reunited victims with their treasure?
Oh, and did he hide his cape
under his Clark Kent coat
and if it ever rode up and bunched,
did the staff at the *Daily Planet* snicker
and mutter "Quasimodo" as he passed?

I suppose that like all of us he muddled
as best he could through the constraints
of the quotidian, but however he managed it,
his last changing room is now hauled away.
He's older now, a step or two slower
on the sprint to strip and transform,
and learning with the rest of us
that our refuges, our struggles
at self-conversion,
never entirely adequate,
vanish with the years,
and that we'll wear to the end the costume
time has tailored to our measure.

Invasion of the Body Snatchers (Then and Now)

The bus passed slowly, glimpsed faces stolid,
as if corpses staring from a hearse.
Health Inspector Donald Sutherland
sensed something off, as did I, though just a kid,
and I turned and watched those around me
watching the screen silently, impassively,
mere husks, maybe, of the neighbors I knew,
gone cold and extraplanetary inside,
making me fear sleep.

Aging now, my own health inspector,
I stare at the husk in the mirror
and sense something within it terminally off,
alien but an intimate from the beginning,
burrowing from the first, ready at last,
whether I wake or sleep, to snatch
what was never really mine to keep.

The Sciences

Contact Tracing

Well before they pulled the tubes, placed him
on the gurney, draped him with a sheet,
and wheeled him to a quiet gray room
lacking landscape paintings and monitors,
they'd determined that he'd picked up the Covid
while getting fitted for tortoiseshell bifocals
to replace the pair his puppy had chewed
after he'd left them on the couch to answer
the phone call from an overseas scammer
(working overtime to send rupees home
to his struggling kin in Madhya Pradesh)—
the pup, a Wheaton mix, was a rescue,
found wandering the streets of San Diego,
and glimpsed online by his wife, yearning
for a dog ever since their frisky black lab
had happened on a sun-basking copperhead.
The technician fitting his glasses
had caught a dry cough from her boyfriend,
who satisfying a yen for a Krispy Kreme
chatted in line with a man who'd shared sushi
three nights before with a friend just back
from a business trip to Beijing (taken on short notice
when a colleague had to bail after his daughter failed
the bar and talked of hurting herself), where
he and a mid-level manager from Wuhan
took a selfie together over classic gin-fizzes,
the mid-level manager having strolled
through an open-air market in his native city
a few days earlier, freely sampling its delicacies,
including a bit of Cave Nectar bat, not typically part
of the Wuhan cuisine, but available now and again
for those tempted to try something exotic, the bat,
like all in its species, holding, one expert stated,
a "robust and long-term evolutionary relationship"
with viruses for what may be millions of years,
viruses nearly as old as the planet,
which all know took shape with the Big Bang,
which itself, many still believe, took shape
in the mind of God. How that mind took shape
is beyond the reach of this contact trace.

The Neanderthal in Me

> "Neanderthals have contributed between 1-4% of the DNA of humans of Eurasian descent."
> —Smithsonian Institution

Finishing the *Smithsonian* article,
I stare intently at my reflection,
see that to the discerning eye
the supraorbital ridge is more prominent
than most, the nose broader,
the head flatter. Short and burly,
I note my heavy shoulders, large, furred pecs,
thick calves, and conclude
that I don't need to send a spit sample
off to some Heredity dot Com
to know that I must be off the charts,
Neanderthal DNA-wise.

The Mayflower Society
and the First Families of Virginia
now strike me as parvenus, arrivistes,
given to laughable pretensions.
So their forebears fought French and Indians,
mine wielded wooden club and spear against mammoths
in the days when hominids were truly hominids.

I'd been contemplating a nap,
but suddenly feel the urge to hunt and gather,
to roam the steppes, woodlands, and deep ravines
of the park. I eschew the elevator, bound down
six flights, trot through the lobby,
giving the doorman lounging under the awning
a low, guttural greeting, and hit the pavement,
walking rapidly on the balls of my feet
with a hunched rolling gait,
sniffing the air, scenting, as if for the first time,
the breath of the season, the pungent aroma
of all that has been lost.

Doing What Comes Naturally

The soft spines of caterpillars
are at once landing strips
and rich soil for certain wasps,
ripe to sow their crop of eggs.
They alight gently, extend ovipositors,
puncture and inject.

Hatched before long, their young feed
on the body and blood of their living host
till they take wing, leaving a husk,
desiccated and dying, that never knows
it too was born to float and swim
in air, its agony incalculable
by any means known to man.

"I cannot persuade myself,"
said Darwin, "that a beneficent
and omnipotent God would have
designedly created parasitic wasps
with the express intention of their feeding
in the living bodies of caterpillars."

There are innumerable species
of Parasitoid wasps, all adept
at destruction, and it does indeed
seem unlikely that so many
could have boarded, two-by-two,
for the passage to Ararat.

Thus, on our own, we contemplate
the incomprehensible nature
of nature and its processes of selection.

Doctor Josef Mengele, *der Weisse Engle*
(of the classification *Todesengle*),
argued that choosing a child for liquidation
would not be "humanitarian"
without permitting the mother to witness,
explaining, "That is why I send the mother

and child to the gas ovens together."
Thirty-four years later, Mengele drowned
off the coast of Brazil when a clot forming
over time grew large enough to block
the anterior cerebral artery, causing
an ischemic stroke.

The Orb Weaver

"If design govern in a thing so small"
—Robert Frost

It weaves at night, spinning a web
from itself, spider silk, fine strands,
strong as steel, yet sufficiently pliant
to snare the passing fly. They vibrate
only slightly with its frantic wings.
Just before dawn, the spider dines,
drinks dew off the spun filament,
and reels the web back into itself
through spinnerets at the very tips
of its abdomen, miniscule spigots
fitted precisely to the silk glands inside.
In time, it is whole again, and rests
from daylight till dark.

Much potential for allegory here—
the serial seducers, the artful demagogues,
the Eternal Imprisoner of Lost Souls
all pouring their very selves into their tasks—
the stuff of Miltonic blank verse, couplets
by Pope, blues by Holiday. Perhaps.
Or, merely one more incarnation
of design shaped meticulously by time
and signifying little, less, or nothing at all.

Soft Inheritance and Hard

The tide rises, wave on wave,
and the piper's spindly legs stretch
and strain in the rushing surf, steadying him,
as he grips the shore and peers
for the mollusks, the grubs and the worms
his probing beak will poke and pierce.
Over time, the legs lengthen
with his effort and he stands firm
in yet higher waters, while the beak,
narrowing and sharpening to a fine point
in the endless striving for the next meal,
increasingly serves him well. Were he to dwell
on such matters, he'd be pleased to know
the eggs his mate hatches in the tall grasses
hold pipers whose legs will be longer,
beaks keener, because of his labors,
much as the blacksmith, hammering at his anvil
through the sweaty years, knows the right arm
of his infant son has been forged to bulge with muscle.

Thus the acquired becomes the innate and the gains pass
inexorably from parent to child in a "Soft Inheritance,"
say some. Would it were so. In fact, inheritance is hard,
wired into genes and impervious to efforts of piper
or blacksmith, oblivious to need, indifferent to yearning.
So, as my son, nestled in the crook of my elbow, frowns
and whimpers with each early glimpse of the waiting world,
one might almost think he knows how ill-equipped
to face its tides and blows his father's legacy has left him.

The Brain, They Say, is Built to Forget

> "Every species that has a memory forgets."
> —Michael Andersen, University of Cambridge Neuroscience

Little finds its way along the neural network
from short-term memory storage in the hippocampus
to the long-term vaults of the cortex. It's Darwinian,
—survival of only the recollections fittest
to help us face the lurking future.
You must remember only that the lion will pounce,
not that it was on a twelve-inch Zenith
with rabbit-ears that you watched the gazelle
get torn apart. Yet, you recall each catch
in your dad's voice the day, forty years past,
when he called to tell you mom was dead.
You recall that as you clutched the phone,
too choked to speak, Elvis, on WNEW,
was singing "Don't Be Cruel," that you'd eaten
a hamburger and fries for lunch and wore
a blue pin-striped shirt, with a gravy stain
above the pocket, a trace of the meatloaf
she'd made the last time you were home.
That's all still there for you, although she isn't—
she's instead as gone as any scudding cloud
that afternoon at 3:10, which you'll always know
as the moment your phone rang.

The necessary detail was that she died.
From it you could predict that, soon or late,
loved ones vanish and you could learn to brace
for sharp-toothed loss that creeps ever closer
through the high weeds of what seems an endless
savanna of sunshine and mild breezes.

So, why still recall that breaking voice, that shirt,
that song, an ice cream truck's chimes in the street,
the barking of a dog, a slammed door in the next house,
the profitless facts of forty years past?
Are you terminally unfit, your brain too clogged
with sentiment's detritus for your survival

in this world of clawing and ripping, or are you merely,
like most, more human than your circuitry,
as you carry throughout your fleeting time,
a trove of no special value,
yet too precious to leave behind?

Molyneux's Problem

William Molyneux, man of the Enlightenment,
seeking the boundaries of the empirical,
asked if one born blind, taught by touch
the cube and sphere, might, with eyes
newly brought to life, perceive by sight alone
which object his hand had known as cornered,
which as round.

My friend, sightless from birth, married his classmate
in British Romantics, quite lovely, as we all told him,
though he'd say he just *knew* she walked in beauty,
like the night.

In their third year together, doctors gave him vision.
At last, after the bandages and the blur, he saw her
in sharp outline, leaning toward him, smiling gently.
He recoiled and never faced her again without flinching.
Neither reason nor intuition could tell us just what
he'd expected.

Gene Therapy and its Discontents

He was twelve, born deaf, but science had undone
nature's glitch, and he'd gained a fifth sense.
Not wanting to seem ungrateful, he'd grinned
and signed that there was no sound he didn't like.
In fact, there were few sounds that he found bearable.
Music, sometimes, was one, though he couldn't
make out the purpose of all the plinking and plucking,
the blowing, bowing, and banging.
But most people evidently enjoyed the clamor, so
he would bob with the rest to the throbbing beat.
They were watching him, and it seemed the thing to do,
and they smiled at him, and he would smile back.
Birdsongs were nice, but never so nice
as when he'd merely read of them, the same
with brooks, with leaf-stirring breezes,
with the solid contact of bat and ball.
There was so much noise! Jackhammers,
backhoes, chainsaws, chippers, even the crackling
of a crunched-up candy-bar wrapper and the strange
click and clip of the barber's blades at his scalp.
He signed of them all, his long fingers swift, balletic,
dancing their lie of unalloyed gratitude.

It was too late for him to speak words.
Nor could his brain shape into sense
those spoken to him. The staccato spewing
from behind curling lips made him yearn to pull
the soft blanket of silence back over his ears,
but he knew it was also too late for that.

A few years after, he came across *Frankenstein*
on TV, watched (with closed captioning) to its conclusion,
and heaved sobs that sounded like distant storm.

Dolce far Niente

> "A substantial percentage of participants opted to voluntarily self-administer an electric shock rather than sit quietly [for fifteen minutes] with their thoughts."
> Result of experiment on boredom by the Department of Psychology, University of Virginia.

To sit with one's thoughts for fifteen minutes
in a bare room with nothing at hand
but an electric prod on a table,
is harsh, even as experiments go.
No wonder so many passed the hard time
zapping the flesh. The jolts hurt a bit, sure,
but were clearly the less painful option,
whether "self-administered" to arm or leg,
or perhaps even to more sensitive spots,
a prospect which doesn't bear speculation.
And, of course, it was speculation itself
that loomed so menacingly, the unseen
elephant beneath the bare fluorescents—
speculation such as "Do I have any thought
that could possibly please me?" or "Do I own
any thoughts at all?" or "Is telling myself
I'm bored a step back from the abyss?"
Easiest to say, "Any stimulation
is better than none" and let it go at that.

When as a child, I complained that I was bored,
my mother would say, "Hit your head against the wall."
Now I see she was simply trying to protect me.

The Embrace of AGNES

In Cambridge, that afternoon, AGNES held me
while the breeze off the Charles hinted
of summer's passing—a brief encounter,
decades ago but never forgotten.
Immediately my vision blurred and yellowed
and mobility of my cervical spine diminished.
Stiffened at each joint, I found my feet uncertain
of where they stood, my hands slow and bumbling.

I'd never known such feelings.
I seemed suddenly older,
enfolded in AGNES' firm grasp,
and it was more than I was ready for.
Fleeing from AGNES, I raced down four flights,
felt the riverside path firmly underfoot,
swung my arms, flexed my fingers, strode freely,
and watched whitecaps rise vividly
and drop crisply in the choppy flow,
as scudding clouds sped in the bright blue
above my hurrying youth.

An undergrad in the grip of the Age Gain Now
Empathy System, an "aging suit" experiment,
I'd become briefly my grandfather,
whose hobbling, narrowing life
was a daily progress from the morning paper
at the kitchen table to the couch and CNN,
and then again to bed with its restless hours
and muddled memories. I'd gained less empathy
than terror. Alert now to the System
that embraces us all in an eternal experiment
of dubious success, I'd feared for myself.

C'mon, Get Happy!

> "The research found that among great composers like Beethoven, a 37% increase in sadness led to, on average, one extra major composition."
> —Arthur Brooks, in *Build the Life You Want: The Art and Science of Getting Happier*

The day we buried my dad, the gravesite survey
showed my sadness was up twenty-three percent.
Could have been higher, but Dad was a drinker
and quick with the back of his hand. Slow with a buck,
though, when his kids begged for a Snickers or a Coke.
And the sunshine, the smell of new grass and rich dirt,
the chirping of birds in a cypress, the matched pair
of boilermakers I slugged back with some Bojangles
sausage biscuits that morning all must have also shaved
a few points. Can't choose feelings, can you? Still,
just fourteen percent more and my latest, "Papa's Gone,
but Your Big Sugar-Daddy's Standin' Right Here, Girl,"
might have really climbed the charts. You know,
I could have had maybe a bit more heavy riffing
on grief motifs to touch the heart and soul. Oh well,
after we shovel the soil on Mom, I'll definitely
have a major hit on my hands.

“All the reflections seemed to move in unison.”

Astronomer Brian Greene, theorist of parallel universes, recalling himself as a child reflected endlessly in the facing mirrors of his bedroom.

The operative word is “seemed,”
because it does take time
for the images to volley endlessly
into infinite recession,
each marking the past
of a peering, recollected being,
each a token of elsewheres
gone, going, or impending,
each near kin to our fleeting here.

The barber’s long straight-blade,
stropped with strenuous care,
cut smoothly through the thin layer
of cream spread across my nape,
slicing the month-old crop
of fine, downy hair right to the skin.
I was twelve, unsettled each visit
with watching my multipliable self,
mirrored innumerably, front wall and back,
raising and straightening its neck
to receive the touch of ten,
twenty—for all I could tell, as I stared,
a thousand razors, each, it seemed,
in a world of its own in a stream
of worlds without end.

Then, one day I watched as one razor
in the infinite row reached round
to one throat and drew blood
bright and flowing as the scarlet stripe
revolving perpetually behind glass
in the barbershop pole.

When the cape was swept from me
and my un-slit neck, I rose from the chair
as if reprieved; and outside, vertiginous,
dazed with what I saw of possibility,
I blinked in the shine of one sun
at countless silicate grains glistening
in the pavement of one street, one city.

Quantum Entanglement

> "No reasonable definition of reality could be expected to permit this."
> —Albert Einstein

Unreasonably, unexpectedly, and undeniably,
no matter the separating avenues or light years,
change in an entwined photon rouses its partner.
Picture a coin flipped to heads on Earth turning
its mate on Alpha Centauri to tails. So strange,
this "spooky action at a distance," as Einstein calls it.
Hard, though, for those with a rage for relation
not to analogize. The high school physics student
carving his crush's initials linked with his own
into his classroom desk can't quite unconvince himself
that while reading Whitman or Keats down the hall
she doesn't feel her fingertips tingling lightly.
The thwarted lover who reads the science mags
chuckles bitterly, "Oh, yeah, Quantum Entanglement,
too damn real. Some evenings, just at six here
in New York, a stirring at my dick tells me
that right then, midnight in Paris, she's coiling
in a Left Bank bedroom with that bastard she ran off with."

But, reasonably, we should expect no true analogies
to rise from these uncanny hookups of subatomic particles,
for all experience tells us we isolates can never entangle
so intimately as to bridge the separating spaces,
be they infinite or infinitesimal.

An Astronaut Sees Forever

> "For years, Space Shuttles emptied their septic tanks during missions: astronaut urine, instantly transformed into glimmering snowflake clouds, is reputed to be among the most beautiful visions in space."
> —Raffi Khatchadourian, "The Trash Nebula"

Two hundred and fifty miles up,
the weather forever clear,
there's no end to what you can see.
A billion trillion, (or is it a trillion billion?) stars,
each on the move, heading farther
and farther from you, from each other,
and from the infinitesimal motherless womb
that once pulsed with all. Nothing you see is ours.

You're a quarter of a thousand miles closer
to the neighbors—Mars, Venus, and Mercury—
but see neither hedge to trim nor yard to mow,
not a leaf of grass for a Whitman to pluck
and chew meditatively, some sweet strand
telling him each is part of the lasting all
and that all is luckier than we supposed.
No one's home.

From your capsule outpost of progress
you gaze in troubled surmise at vacancy,
the endless spaces and desert places,
floating with you, circling without tether,
and you feel a penetrating frost. You sigh,
dog paddle weightlessly to the septic tank,
and drain it. The trail of glimmering waste
you leave as you lower your raised lever
marks that you were here, then carried off
with the general drift of things.

Desert Places Indeed

They couldn't scare him, Frost claimed,
with their spaces, vast and vacant,
between stars bereft and barren,
for inside, where the lack of meaning is,
stretched a desolateness no less fearsome.
Yesterday, though, a billion light years away,
a neutron star, more than a billion tons
to the heaped teaspoon, vanished utterly,
a black hole's pull its undoing.
"Just a big, quick gulp, and gone,"
said a learn'd astronomer, a gorging
begetting as much energy as all light visible.
Yet, no one had said, "Let there be blind megaforce
in a cosmic Sahara endlessly churning,
devouring itself, growing itself, devoid
of sound, lacking fury, signifying nothing
but that it is." This might scare even Frost,
were he still here to be scared.

Acknowledgments

My thanks to the editors of the journals in which the following poems first appeared:

The Delmarva Review: "A Room With No View"

The Hudson Review: "The Neanderthal in Me"

Vox Populi: "Contact Tracing,"

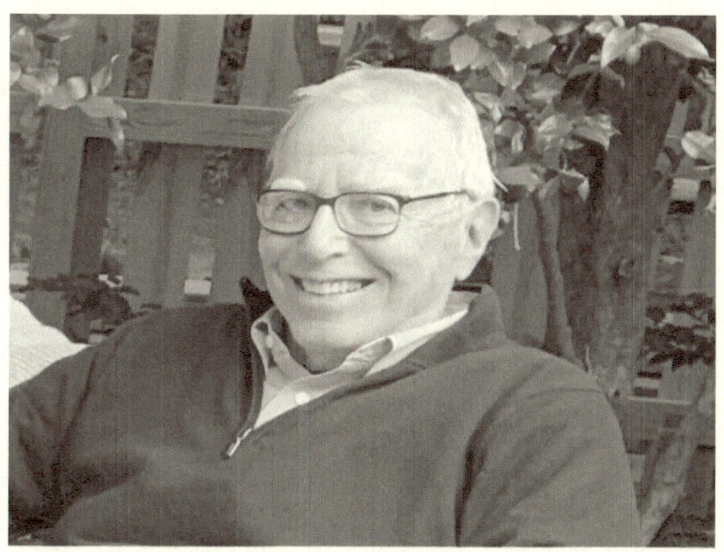

About the Author

Allen Stein's poems have been published in over thirty journals, among them *The Hudson Review*, *Poet Lore*, *Willow Springs*, *Salmagundi*, *New Ohio Review*, *Southern Poetry Review*, and *Valparaiso Poetry Review*. He has twice been nominated for the Pushcart Prize. His first poetry collection, *Your Funeral is Very Important to Us*, was a semi-finalist in the University of Wisconsin poetry series' Brittingham and Felix Pollak Prize in Poetry competition and was published in 2019 by Main Street Rag. His second collection, *Unsettled Subjects:New Poems on Classic American Literature*, was published in 2020 by Broadstone.

www.ingramcontent.com/pod-product-compliance
Lightning Source LLC
LaVergne TN
LVHW051016080826
845145LV00009B/2660

* 9 7 8 1 9 6 3 6 9 5 6 3 2 *